Bob McCurdy

Carving
Faces

A Step-by-Step System

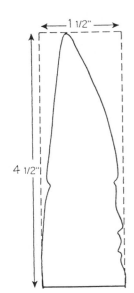
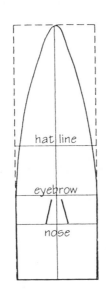
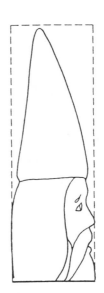
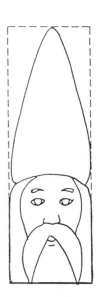

by Bob McCurdy

INCLUDING A SPECIAL SECTION ON
CAPTURING VARIOUS FACIAL EXPRESSIONS

Wm Caxton Ltd
12037 Hwy 42
Ellison Bay, WI 54210
1997

Published by:

Wm Caxton Ltd
12037 Highway 42
Ellison Bay, WI 54210

(414) 854-2955

Printed in the United States of America.

10 9 8 7 6 5 4 3 2 1

Library of Congress Cataloging-in-Publication Data

McCurdy, Robert, 1939-
    Carving faces : a step-by-step system / by Bob McCurdy.
       p. cm.
    "Including a special section on capturing various facial expressions."
    ISBN 0-940473-36-4 (pbk. : alk. paper)
    1. Wood-carving--Technique. 2. Face in art. 3. Head in art.
    I. Title.
    TT199.7.M3275 1997
    736'.4--dc21   97-4284
                                                                              CIP

ISBN# 0-940473-36-4 pbk

This book is set in a version of Times Roman type chosen for its readability and attractiveness; it is printed on acid-neutral paper bound in sewn signatures and is intended to provide a very long useful life.

The cover design and many of the illustrations were done by Donna Wold.

The photographs in the book were taken by W. Joseph Christiansen.

To my parents

Russell & Virginia McCurdy

who encouraged their sons

in all their artistic endeavors.

Table of Contents

Introduction

Most wood carvers have difficulty carving faces. In seminars on carving figures or caricatures, even advanced carvers usually focus on the problems of doing the human face. In my discussions with other carvers, the bulk of the conversation always seems to be about techniques for carving the face, and usually I am most interested in how they approach this task.

Over the years, I have developed a step-by-step approach to carving faces. This system can demystify the task and turn the process of carving faces into the most enjoyable part of doing any figure. Once you master the basic techniques of carving faces, the real fun can begin — finding ways of capturing various facial expressions.

Most of this book is devoted to explaining my system for carving faces. I do this by showing how to carve four different kinds of faces, beginning with the simplest and proceeding to the more challenging — first, a bearded male face; next, a male face without facial hair; then a female face; and, finally, a child's face. In the last part of the book, some of the ways of carving particular expressions are demonstrated.

My system is well-defined by now, at least in my own mind, but it is always open to refinement and modification. Just the other day I discovered a subtle change that improved the way I do my initial cuts when blocking in a nose on a carving. I teach carving both through organizations and on a private, contractual basis, and I have shown this system to hundreds of people. Those who have tried it have found it helpful, and most have also found that the system helps them get much more enjoyment from wood carving. I hope that it will have the same effect for you.

Chapter 1
Sharpening

If you read twenty-five books on carving, you'll learn twenty-five different methods of sharpening your tools. So — let's go for number twenty-six, though briefly. However, before discussing the actual techniques of sharpening, a couple of remarks are in order.

First, it is often said that a dull knife is a dangerous knife. Actually, any knife can be dangerous when used without caution, but there is some truth to the idea that a dull knife is more dangerous than a sharp one. One of the main objects in using any tool is to be in control of the tool, to be able to make the tool do what you want it to do. You can control a sharp knife more easily than a dull one. The duller your knife, the more force you must use to make it cut, and the more force needed, the less control you have. Carving with a sharp knife is easier, and therefore safer and less frustrating. Also, a sharp knife usually yields better results in the final product.

Second, though my method of sharpening works well for me and has been developed over a long process of trial and error, it is not necessarily the best method that could be. If I find a better method tomorrow, I'll switch to it in a blink. I try to make a living carving wood, so I need a sharpening system that is quick and efficient, and I'd rather be carving than sharpening anyway. Also,

I move around a lot, so I need equipment that is compact and portable.

I rely on a fine-grit diamond stone for initial sharpening. Then, once I have a sharp cutting edge, I use a very-fine-grit ceramic stone to polish and smooth the cutting edge. The importance of polishing the cutting edge of a tool cannot be over emphasized, because an effective cutting edge has to be both sharp and smooth. In sharpening a tool, one actually puts scratches in the blade's metal. These scratches create drag when the tool cuts into the wood, thus requiring more force to be applied. By polishing the blade (and thus reducing the scratches), one can significantly reduce the friction between the blade and the wood.

When you do the actual sharpening (working the blade on the stone) there are a few important things to keep in mind. First, if you haven't sharpened a knife before, it may feel awkward at first. Like any new skill, sharpening requires practice to develop real skill and coordination. Hang in there. You'll acquire the skill more quickly than you think.

It is important to keep the length of the cutting edge of the knife blade flat against the stone. That is, the blade you want to sharpen should not be tipped either up or down. Otherwise, you will quickly start to round the shape of the knife blade. Of course, if the blade is already curved (either convex or concave), you'll want to work with that shape when you apply the blade to the stone.

In sharpening a carving tool, you want a fine edge rather than a blunt edge. To do that, raise the back edge of the blade (the edge you are not trying to sharpen) slightly (about 6-10 degrees — see Figure 1-1), and work the tool back and forth across the stone (see Figure 1-2). Also, it is important to work both sides of the blade equally. Therefore, work one side of the blade edge on the stone for a while, then flip it over and work the opposite side of the edge.

Figure 1-1

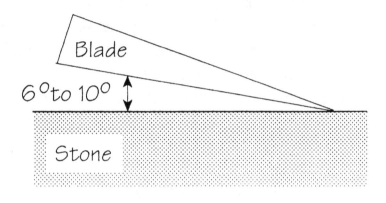

Figure 1-2

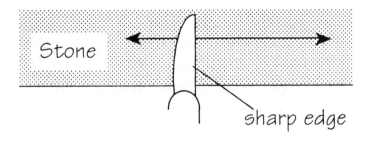

I apply a fair amount of pressure to the blade as I hold it against the stone. If you use a diamond stone, sharpening usually requires only a few licks on each side of the blade to acquire a sharp initial edge (unless the knife was miserably dull to begin with). Once I have that sharp initial edge, I seldom return to using a coarse stone, but instead maintain a good keen edge using the ceramic stone, which adds to the polish on the surface of the metal. Thus, when the knife begins to feel as if it needs a sharpening touchup, I return to the ceramic stone. The idea here is to not let the blade get really dull.

When working in my studio, I take the sharpening process one step further. After using the very-fine-grit ceramic stone, I polish the edges on my carving tools with a buffing wheel mounted on a bench grinder, using a very fine polishing compound. (I like to use a product called ZAM). This gives my carving tools a mirror-smooth finish and all but completely eliminates the scratches produced by sharpening.

However, a word of caution about this buffing procedure is in order — use a light touch, and don't overdo it. While you are polishing the metal you are also removing metal, and it is easy to round the cutting edge to a point where you have to go back to step one, sharpening with the diamond stone, to restore the blade's keen edge. Also, if you overdo the buffing process, you will have to resharpen more frequently, and you eventually will wear the knife blade down so much that you cannot use it, and then you'll need to replace it.

When I'm not in my studio, I use an old-fashioned leather strop treated with polishing compound to buff the blade. It fits easily into my toolbox.

I am often asked how often a knife needs to be sharpened. You should sharpen a knife whenever it feels dull. After a while, you'll be able to tell when it's time to touch up a blade by how it's handling (for example, if you need to use more force). You should also be able to tell by the results you produce (for example, if your cuts are not clean and precise). And, after sharpening a tool that needs it, you should notice a difference in the way it feels and performs.

Some woods dull tools more quickly than others, and, oddly enough, they are not always the harder woods. Thus, how frequently you will have to sharpen your tools will depend to some degree on the kind of wood you are working with. For example, we have a wood called white cedar (though it's not a true cedar) here in Door County, Wisconsin; it is also called arborvitae. It is softer than most pines, but it dulls a blade more quickly than most of the other woods I carve. It will dull even the carbide saw blade on my table saw more quickly than other woods. I asked the man who sharpens my saw blades why white cedar dulls blades so quickly. He told me that some trees absorb and retain more minerals in the cells of their wood than do others, and white cedar is one of those woods. Thus, it seems to be the minerals that are actually part of the wood that dull the blades and damage the metal.

So much for sharpening. On to carving faces.

Chapter 2
The Human Head — Shape, Proportions, and Basic Anatomy

Before actually carving faces, you need to consider the basic form of the human head, so that you have a better idea of what you are trying to accomplish.

If you look down on the head from directly above, you immediately see that its outline is shaped rather like an egg (see Figure 2-1). The nose protrudes from that outline as a nearly triangular shape, and, if you draw bisecting lines off the sides of the front of the face you'll see that they intersect at approximately a 90-degree angle. When first attempting to do faces, many carvers fail to shape the front of the head to this oval contour. Instead, they do the face on an almost flat surface, which may be easier to carve, but doesn't look realistic.

Looking at the top view of the human head, you should notice a couple of details about the ears. First, the ears protrude outward from the sides of the head; second, the ears are located behind the mid-line.

Now notice that, looked at from the front, the basic form of the head as a whole is also an egg shape (see Figure 2-2). In most cases, the neck is considerably narrower than the head, and this is more pronounced in women and in children than in adult males.

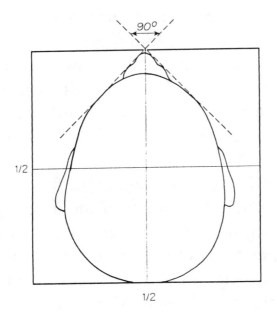

Figure 2-1

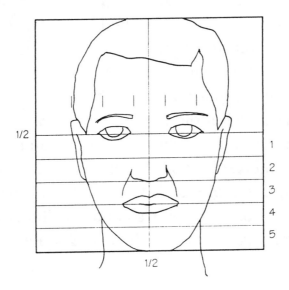

Figure 2-2

9

If we bisect the oval front view of the head both vertically and horizontally and then divide the horizontal line into fifths (see Figure 2-2), we see that each fifth is approximately equal to the width of an eye. Also, the distance between the eyes is about equal to the width of an eye. Thus, the eyes are located just above the horizontal line in the second and fourth spaces on the first horizontal line shown in Figure 2-2.

If we also divide the lower half of the front view of the head into fifths, we see that the bottom of the nose is located about two-fifths of the way down from the center line, and the mouth is located about three-fifth's of the way down, allowing the chin to occupy the remaining area. The length of the ears is approximately equal to the length of the nose.

Unless you have studied the proportions of the human face before, there may be some surprises here. One of them is how much of the face is located below the horizontal center, though if you take into account the eyebrows, the forehead area, and the hairline, the proportions balance out. Many artists use "eye-widths" to measure various proportions of the head (e.g., the length of the nose, the width of the bottom of the nose, the width of the mouth, etc.). I prefer to use the system of horizontal and vertical dividing lines shown in Figures 2-1 and 2-2 and then do what looks right after that. But, if you are not comfortable with my system, or if you feel the need for more precise and specific measurements, I recommend investing in some of the very good art books that are available.

Finally, if we look at the human head in side view and again bisect the form both horizontally and vertically, we can also see much of what was observed in the top and front views:

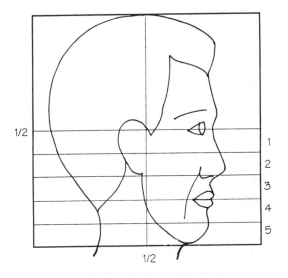

Figure 2-3

1. The ears are located behind the vertical median, and they are the same length as the nose.

2. The center of the eye is above the horizontal median.

3. The top of the mouth is located about three-fifths of the way down the lower face, and the chin occupies the rest of the lower face.

However, there are also a couple of new observations that can be made from the side view:

4. Notice that there is an indentation at the top of the nose where the nose bone joins the skull. This feature usually is more prominent in adult males than in adult females or in children, but it exists in virtually all faces.

5. Notice that there is an indentation between the lower lip and the main portion of the chin. In most faces, the chin below that indentation protrudes forward to a point about even with the lips.

Later, as you progress from one face to another, you will note the various and sometimes subtle differences between adult male faces, adult female faces, and children's faces. But, for now, we are concerned only with an overview of the basic shape and the proportions of the human head. Of course, there is a vast array of different sizes and shapes of eyes, noses, mouths, and ears, to say nothing of chins and cheek bones, eyebrows and hairlines, facial lines and dimples, and on and on. And there is also the whole subject of facial expressions, which are determined by contraction or relaxation of facial muscles. We will consider facial expressions in some detail in Chapter 8.

As you begin carving faces, you may find yourself returning to this Chapter from time to time to refresh your memory on facial proportions, but this eventually will become second nature to you. However, even now, after having carved hundreds of faces, I still always draw in the vertical center line and locate the placement of the eyebrows above the horizontal center line before I do anything else. I almost always draw in the hairline (and the hat, if the figure has one) before starting on the face itself. This allows me to know the exact size and shape of the face area. Of course, this is my own personal approach to carving faces, and you should experiment to find out what works best for you. If you come up with a better idea, please write to me and share it. I'm always open to new ideas, especially any that help get the job done better.

Chapter 3
Blanks

Let's make it as easy on ourselves as possible by cutting some blanks before we actually start in on the carving.

A blank is simply a piece of wood that has been preshaped by cutting off some of the wood to form a rough outline of the final product.

I prefer basswood (*Tilia americana*), which is also sometimes called linden or lime wood, for carving, partly because it is abundantly available where I live, but mostly because it is a wonderful medium for carving. It is softer than most other hardwoods, and, because of its close grain, one can achieve marvelous detail in carving it with little fear of the wood breaking or splitting. However, in some parts of the country, basswood is either not available or not so desirable. For some reason, northern basswood seems to be much better for carving than basswood grown further south. I can attest to that difference from my own experience.

Fortunately, there are other woods almost as nice to carve as northern basswood that should be readily available wherever you live. For example, in the Rocky Mountain states, you will have access to aspen, and cottonwood is available throughout most of North America. On the West Coast, sugar pine is a good local wood for carving. East of the Mississippi River, eastern white pine is often available. In the deep south, gum and some cypress woods work very well for carving. In short, you'll find some kind of local wood suitable for carving just about anywhere in North America.

The ideal tool for cutting out a blank shape is a band saw, though a scroll saw can also be used. In lieu of power tools, a coping saw will do the job. Coping saws are quite inexpensive and are available in most hardware stores.

I generally draw a side profile of the piece to be carved on a block of wood (other than a blank) cut to about the size I want, and I usually draw it on a piece of paper before I put it onto the block of wood. In doing so, I include many of the details of the carving-to-be so that I can get a better idea of what it will look like. This gives me a chance to think the whole project through before committing it to the block of wood.

If you're just starting out as a carver, I encourage you to draw your projects on paper first — including front, side, and back views. This will help your brain to consider the carving in three dimensions. Your eyes see things in three dimensions, but it may be difficult at first to translate what you see into a three-dimensional carved figure. By going through the exercise of drawing different views of the head, and then carving the views, your brain gets used to thinking in three-dimensional terms. When I teach beginning classes, I always show the class a finished figure and ask them to draw it in all three perspectives; this helps to get their brains thinking in terms of translating between three dimensional figures and two-dimensional sketches.

Begin by drawing the exact dimensions of the block of wood you are going to use. In this case, you are going to carve a wizard head, so you will be using a piece of wood one and one-half inches wide, one and one-half inches thick, and four and one-half inches long (with the grain of the wood running the long way). Graph paper can be very helpful in this part of the project. Figure 3-1 shows the process of designing a side-profile blank.

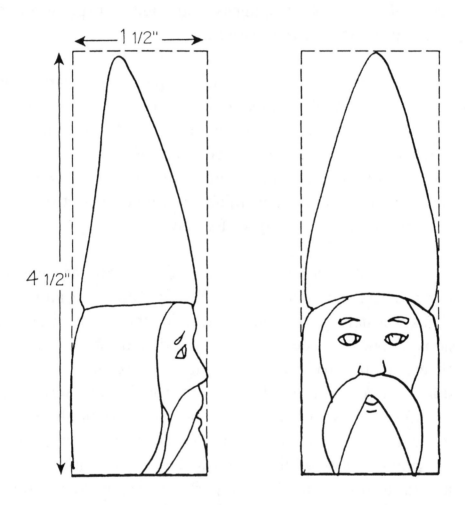

Figure 3-1: The Design of a Carving Blank.

I have chosen the wizard head as a first project partly because the hat is conical and tapered, and that helps to make the figure relatively simple to carve. Figure 3-1 shows both front and side profiles so that you can see what they look like. With other kinds of hats, I often spend as much time carving the hat as I do carving the rest of the head. However, since we're primarily concerned with carving faces in this book, I suggest that you put off doing more complex hats until you have mastered faces.

Once you have laid out the dimensions of the block, you can draw the profile or side view. Note that the profile allows for the nose, but does not include the mouth or eyes. Those will be carved in later, as you progress through the steps. Don't worry about them now.

After you have drawn the profile or side view of the figure on a piece of paper, transfer the profile to the block of wood and cut out the shape. Then, with the front profile surface facing you, draw a center line the full length of the blank. You can either eyeball this line or measure it carefully before drawing it in, whichever suits you best. But, however you establish it, you'll find that the center line (dividing the right half of the head from the left half) is an important reference that will help you to achieve symmetry and balance in the face as you progress with the carving process.

Next, draw in the conical shape of the hat in the front view (see Figure 3-1), and then draw in horizontal lines to mark the positions of the eyebrows and of the bottom of the nose. Finally, you should draw in a line on either side of the center line (between the eyebrow line and the bottom-of-the-nose line) to establish the approximate position, size, and shape of the nose. You will draw in other lines later, but this is all you need for now, and any other lines that you draw in at this point will only be carved away as you shape the head.

If you want to, you can use a saw to cut off the waste wood on the sides of the hat in both front and side views, but that wood will also carve off easily.

You now have your blank of a wizard's head prepared and are ready to start carving it. Detailed instructions about how to proceed on the wizard's head are found in Chapter 4.

*   *   *

There are three other heads — an American Indian head with headdress in Chapter 5, a woman's head in Chapter 6, and a child's head in Chapter 7 — discussed in detail below. As you will see, on some of those figures, the hairdo involves considerably more detail than the simple conical shape of the wizard's hat. Also, on some figures with hats (or headdresses), the hats are much more complicated and challenging to carve than the one on the wizard's head, and there are all sorts of tricks and techniques for carving such hairdos and hats. We'll discuss some of them later on in this book, and you'll learn many others on your own, either through trial and error or from other, more specialized books. However, you should keep in mind that the basic steps for carving the face itself will always remain the same, regardless of any other features you may include in your carvings. Once you have the hang of this step-by-step system, it can be applied to any human face.

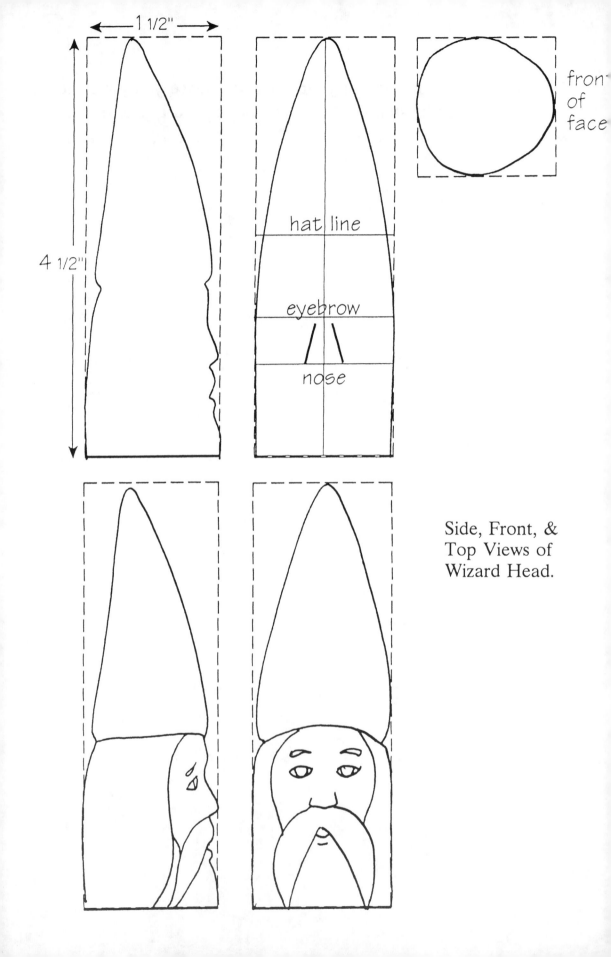

1 1/2"

4 1/2"

hat line

eyebrow

nose

front of face

Side, Front, & Top Views of Wizard Head.

Chapter 4
Carving a Bearded Male Head

As we discussed in Chapter 2, a human head is oval or egg-shaped when seen from the top. Therefore, in doing your initial shaping, you should start by cutting off the corners and rounding off the blank, as seen from the top. Go ahead and rough this shape in, but don't bother to refine it too much at this time. That will occur as you complete the carving. Try to achieve a symmetrical shape.

Once you have taken the corners off, shape the hat portion of the blank into a cone. Next, draw a line around the entire circumference of the head to mark the bottom edge of the hat, allowing space above the eyes for the forehead. Also draw in a horizontal line for the eyebrows and two vertical lines on either side of the center line to mark the sides of the nose. Give yourself room to play with by drawing these lines in broadly. Your blank should now look like the one in Figure 4-1.

Figure 4-1

Next make a stopcut following the line you have just drawn all the way around the head. This cut need not be very deep — a sixteenth of an inch at most — and it should be cut in vertically from the surface. Then cut upward from below that line

Figure 4-2

to make the hat stand out (see Figure 4-2). A hat sits over the hair, so the wood below the hat line should be carved in a bit.

Next, draw in the hairline on either side of the head. Then cut in toward the hairlines (see Figure 4-3) to make the hair stand out. This is a method of carving called "incised relief" which involves cutting a V-shaped groove. Do this by cutting along the hairline with your

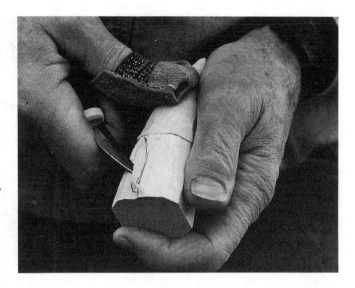

Figure 4-3

blade at an angle and then cutting back on the forward side of that line at an opposing angle so as to make a broad V-shaped groove.

You have now established the position of everything around the face — the hat and the hairline — and are ready to start on the face itself. I always follow this procedure — that is, I get everything set up around the face before I carve in the features.

If you were carving a head with a more complicated hat, you would do exactly the same thing up to the hat, but the hat would then be done separately. I usually do the initial head shape up to the hat, then carve the hat, and only then complete the face.

To start on the facial features, the first step is to block in the nose by making stopcuts on both sides of the nose. Notice the slight curve of these lines, as can be seen in Figure 4-4.

Your next step is to cut in along the eyebrow line at a downward angle and then to remove the wood from the upper cheek region on both sides of the nose. This step forms the nose, the upper part of the eye socket (the supra-orbital ridge), and the upper cheek (see Figure 4-5). You accomplish three things at once with this procedure; you form the sides of the nose, you carve the bottom of the brow, and you establish the top margin of the cheek all at the same time.

Figure 4-4

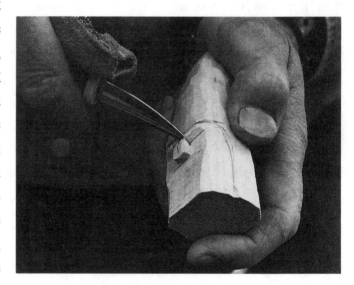

Figure 4-5

Next, carve a small piece off either side of the bottom of the nose to give the bottom of the nose a bit of a V shape (see Figure 4-6). Hardly anybody has a perfectly flat nose on the bottom. Make sure that your knife is sharp before doing this step, since you will be cutting across the grain. A dull knife may cause the wood to tear or break.

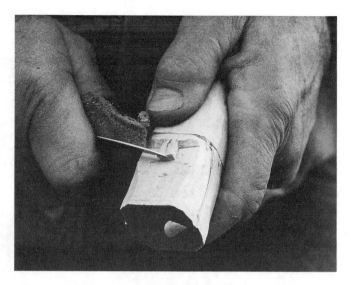

Figure 4-6

As we discussed in Chapter 2, the nose has a V shape as it protrudes from the face, when seen from above. To give your wizard's nose that shape, you need to carve off a triangular

Figure 4-7

chunk of wood (see Figure 4-7) from the each side of the length of the nose — notice that you'll want to make stopcuts in line with the brow ridges to keep those cuts from carrying beyond the line of the eyebrows. Then cut a wide V indentation a the top of the nose where the eyebrows start (see Figure 4-8). This forms the indentation between the top of the nose and the brow ridges that also was mentioned above in Chapter 2.

Figure 4-8

To give the nose its final shape, you need to establish the external shape of the nostrils. To do this, first cut in along the sides of the nose at a shallow sloping angle, then twist the knife to cut upward in the wood (see Figure 4-9). This forms the flare of the nostrils on either side of the bottom of the nose.

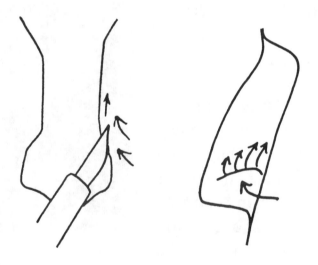

Figure 4-9

Hurray, you've made a nose! I like to experiment with nose shape, and I often try differently shaped noses on my figures. It is remarkable how any change in the shape of a nose can affect the appearance of the entire face, and as you gain experience, one of the ways in which you can make each of your carvings distinctive is by adjusting their noses.

You are now ready to proceed to the next step in carving the wizard's head. First, draw in the lines outlining the moustache and the top of the beard. Then, when you're satisfied with the design, go back over those lines with the knife, making the stopcuts (see Figure 4-10). Next, working from the nose outward toward the hairline on either side, cut downward to the stopcuts to make the beard and moustache stand out a little from the cheeks. You will also want to leave the moustache a little higher than the beard where it overlaps it, so that the moustache will stand out from it more. You do this by carving the beard down a bit.

Figure 4-10

I always work the top edge of the moustache first, then carve upward to form the underside of the moustache, which also stages

27

the area for the mouth (see Figure 4-11). In making these cuts, be careful not to split off part of the moustache. If that does happen, try to save the piece and glue it back on. The only other alternative is to go deeper and recarve the area.

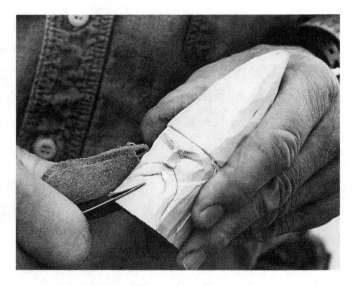

Figure 4-11

You can now proceed to put in the mouth. This is a very simple process and is also one of the most enjoyable, at least in my experience. Place the tip of your knife directly underneath the center of the moustache and then carefully press in to make a stopcut (see Figure 4-12). Next, turn the face around and put in a similar cut from the opposite direction. Finally, pop

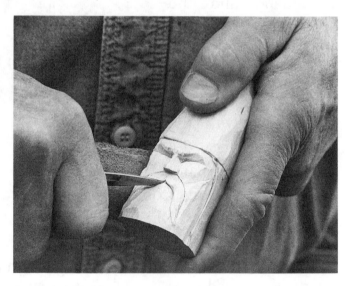

Figure 4-12

out a chip by cutting in and across to form the mouth (see Figure 4-13).

Finally, to complete the mouth and to give it more character, cut a V across the lower line of the mouth to define the line of the lower lip and the beard. If you have a small V-parting tool (that is, a gouge with a V-shaped cutting edge), you can use it to carve in the lower lip (see Figure 4-14), but make sure it is good and sharp before you start to cut.

Figure 4-13

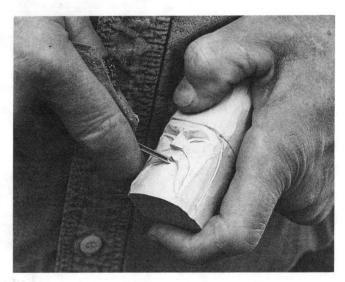

Figure 4-14

You are now ready to put in the eyes. I like to start on the eyes by drawing them in with a pencil before beginning to carve; I want to establish both their location and their exact shape beforehand, since the shape of the eye has a tremendous effect on the expression that emerges. We'll go into the whole subject of eyes and their importance in facial expressions in much greater detail in Chapter 8. For now, we'll draw relaxed, ordinary eyes.

Be especially careful of two things as you draw in the eyes — first, make sure that they are level and even; second, make sure that the two eyes are the same size and shape. You can measure all this, or (if you will pardon the pun) just eyeball it. Note that the top line (which defines the edge of the upper eyelid) should extend past the lower line (which defines the edge of the lower eyelid). If you look at a human eye, you'll see that that's the way it is.

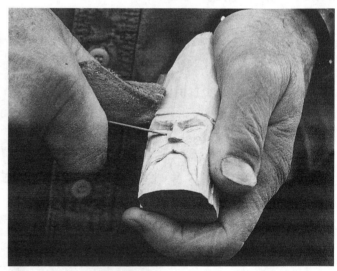

After drawing in both the upper and lower lines that define the eyes and making sure that you are satisfied with their shape and position, use the very tip of the knife blade to make your stopcuts. Cut right into the pencil lines you've drawn (see Figure 4-15).

Figure 4-15

Now, cut back along those stopcuts from the eyeball toward those lines, first at an upward angle along the upper stopcut, then at a downward angle along the lower stopcut. This will not only give you the shape of the eye's perimeter, it will also give you a close proximity to the actual shape of the eyeball itself.

The size, shape, and orientation of the eyes can have a very great affect on the final appearance of a face. Making them rounder or narrower can change the facial expression dramatically. Tilting them slightly downward can have remarkable effect, and changing their overall size even slightly can make them appear very different from one another. This is another region of the face where variations in your style can help to make each carving very distinctive.

To put the final touches to the eye on this figure, make a V cut just below the lower margin of the eye to establish a lower eyelid — I find that a V-parting tool usually works very well for this operation (see Figure 4-16).

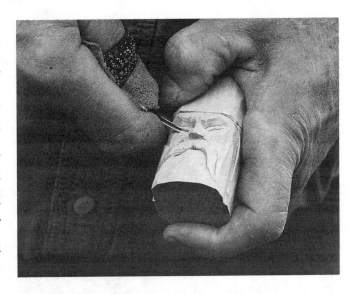

Figure 4-16

On this figure, I often like to add some "crow's feet" (or smile lines, or squint lines, or whatever you prefer to call them) by incising some V-cuts at the outside edges of the eyes. You can also add definition to the eyebrows by cutting in

31

along the top edge of the eyebrows and then twisting the knife to cut upwards and remove enough wood to make the eyebrows stand out a bit more (see Figure 4-17).

Figure 4-17

Congratulations! You've just finished a bearded male head.

However, if you are not quite satisfied with the way your figure looks, you can go back over the head and do whatever touchup or refinement you think necessary. For example, you might want to round off the bottom of the beard or texture the moustache, beard, and hair. I like to use a V-parting tool for this

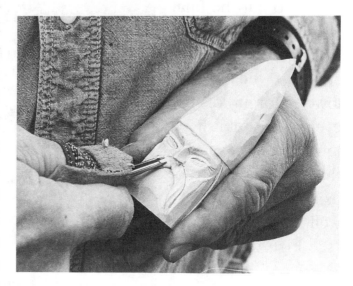

Figure 4-18

procedure (see Figure 4-18). Or you may want to add facial lines, such as a set of vertical frown lines to the forehead between the eyebrows, to give a stern expression to the face, or bags under the eyes, to make the face look older or tired. All of this adds character to the finished product, and we'll discuss many other ways of adding expression to a carved face in the last chapters of this book. However, for now, it is best to confine yourself to relatively simple and subtle facial lines.

If this is your first face, I urge you to sign, date, and keep it. This will allow you to identify it later on for comparison to other carvings that you do later and will help you to see how your carving skills change and develop over time.

*　　*　　*

Before going on to the next phase of carving faces, I suggest that you take a moment to review the steps you went through in carving this face. The basic order of the operations you carried out in carving this head is the same in all the faces that we will discuss here, and you will repeat many of these steps in carving the faces discussed in Chapters 5, 6 and 7.

The steps you followed in carving the wizard's head are as follows:

1. You gave the head an oval shape by cutting off the corners and rounding the head somewhat.

2. You established the position of the lower part of the hat and drew in the hairline.

3. You blocked in the nose by establishing the positions of the sides of the nose and the level of the eyebrows, and established the area for the eye and the upper cheek at the same time.

4. You shaped the nose — first by taking off the edges of the bottom of the nose, then removing excess material on either side of the nose, then forming the bridge of the nose, then notching the top of the nose where it joins the browridge, and finally shaping the flare of the nostrils.

5. You carved the top edge of the moustache and the beard, then carved upward to form the lower line of the moustache, setting the stage for the mouth.

6. You cut in the mouth by making two stopcuts and cutting out a chip, then added the lower lip by cutting a V along the bottom of the mouth.

7. You drew in the eyes and cut upwards and downwards to give the eye its shape, then added a few final touches to the eye by adding a lower lid with a V cut and (perhaps) some squint lines and eyebrows.

And that's it for a bearded face. Of course you can add all sorts of detail by texturing the hair and the beard using a V-parting tool, by adding further lines to the face, or even adding texture or decoration to the wizard's hat — whatever strikes your fancy — but the basic job is done.

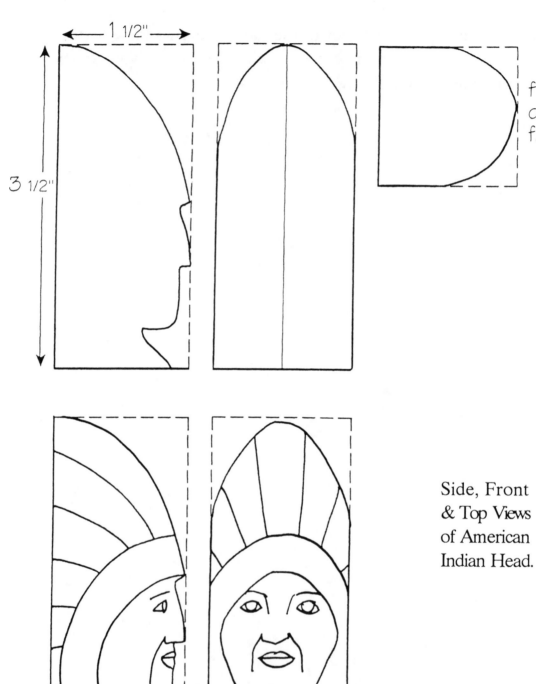

1 1/2"

3 1/2"

front
of
face

Side, Front
& Top Views
of American
Indian Head.

Chapter 5
Carving a Male Head
Without Facial Hair

For this type of head, we'll do a native American Indian with a full headdress. You'll need a block of wood one and one-half inches wide, one and one-half inches thick, and three and one-half inches high, with the grain running the long way. As with the previous head, lay out the side profile and cut out the profile blank. Then draw in a center line and sketch in the shape of the headdress. If you then cut the block to that shape with a saw, you're merely using the saw to remove wood that you will need to remove eventually in any case. And, with this head, the headdress (the feather bonnet) has to be taken into consideration as you start shaping the blank. You will NOT take off the corners and round the back of the head on this head, though you will want to take off the corners and round the front of the head as illustrated in Figure 5-1.

Next, draw in the lines for the headdress on both sides. You can also draw in a line for the eyebrow and draw lines to mark the sides of the nose at this time, since that will help you get all the positions right. You should also draw in a center line. I use a center line on almost everything I carve, whether human figures, animals or birds. It's helpful for achieving balance and symmetry.

Place stopcuts along the headdress reference lines on either side of the head, holding the blade of the knife perpendicular to the wood so that you cut straight in (see Figure 5-1). Then carve that wood away, cutting upwards toward the bonnet (see Figure 5-2), since the bonnet

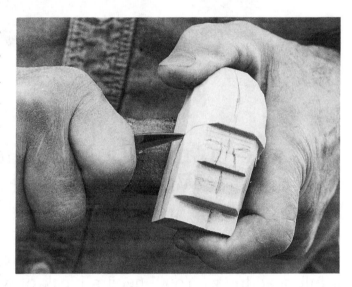

Figure 5-1

sits over the hair and should stand out from it. You may have to go over the stopcuts more than once and work the wood down in stages. You want the bottom edge of the bonnet to protrude out from the hair on either side at least an eighth of an inch. At this stage, however, you should leave the bonnet and proceed with carving the rest of the face. You can return to the bonnet later to add whatever detail you wish, but, for now, focus on the face itself.

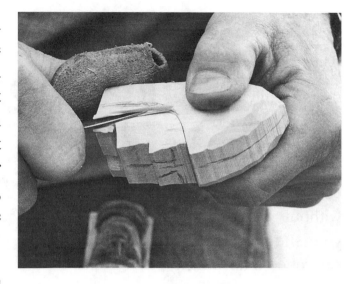

Figure 5-2

As in the wizard head, you should start by blocking in the nose. If you have not already done so, draw in the lines that mark the sides of the nose, the bottom margin of the nose, and the position of the eyebrows; then make the stopcuts and carve out the wood on either side of the nose. Cut the corners off the bottom of the nose at a shallow angle, and cut the edges off both sides of the nose to give the nose its V shape (as seen from above). Next, form the nostrils on either side of the nose by cutting in and twisting the knife upward. I say upward here, even though you probably are holding the piece upside down when carving one side of the nose. So, to carve upward means to carve toward the top of the head, regardless of how you happen to be holding the piece.

All the operations involved in blocking in the nose are closely similar to those described in Chapter 4 for the wizard head, and you may want to review the steps illustrated in Figure 4-5 through Figure 4-9.

However, once you block in the nose, you depart rather dramatically from the steps followed in carving a bearded face. At this point in carving a male head without facial hair, you should draw in reference lines on the cheek area and then make a stopcut at a bit of an angle on either side of the mouth area (see Figure 5-3), starting shallow and making the cut deeper as you progress toward the chin. Next, cut away the wood on the outside of those stopcuts to form the cheeks, while also developing, or staging, the mouth area (see Figure 5-4).

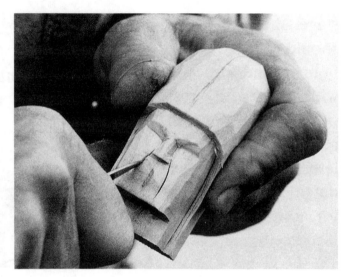

Figure 5-3

Figure 5-4

Notice that the shape of the mouth on this figure is an arc, and you are trying for that shape (or some reasonable facsimile of it) when you set the stage for the mouth. After removing the wood on either side of the mouth, you can carefully shape the arc of the mouth and refine the cheeks a little more (see Figure 5-5). Next, draw in the shape of the lips. You are trying for a somber expression, and so the mouth line will either run straight across or will have a slight downward curve at both ends of it.

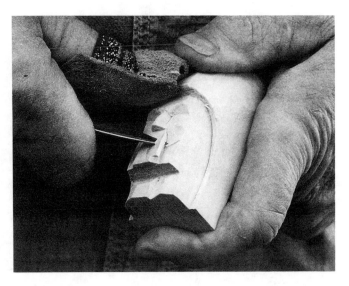

Figure 5-5

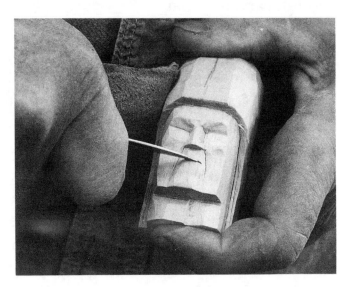

Figure 5-6

To carve the mouth itself, start by making a stopcut across the center line where the upper and lower lips touch (see Figure 5-6), then cut in the upper lip. Begin the stopcut by cutting from the outside toward the center, first on one side, then on the other side (see Figure 5-7). It is very important to get the two sides of the mouth symmetrical at this stage.

Figure 5-7

There is an important general tip about carving that may help you a lot at this point. Carvers have a rule that says that whenever you cut a curvature into wood, the wider the arc, the deeper you must go. Thus, as you carve the curvature of the lips, you should start with a relatively shallow cut at the outside corners and go deeper as the arc becomes wider — in this case, toward the center of the mouth.

You may want to practice this sort of cut on a flat board or on the corner of a scrap piece of wood before you carry it out on an actual carving. That will allow you both to get a feel for how and why this rule works and to practice getting a consistent result with this type of cut before actually carrying it out on your American Indian head.

The next step in forming the mouth is to carve in the lower lip. In carrying out this operation, cut all the way across from one side to the other (see Figure 5-8), again following the rule of going deeper as the arc becomes wider — that is, cut deeper in the center, shallow at the outside edges.

Figure 5-8

Once the basic features of the mouth are carved in — mouth line and lip contours — and you are satisfied with their shape and balance, you may want to add some refinements to the area of the face surrounding the mouth. One particularly effective addition is to carve in the center cleft that extends from just below the nose down to the margin of the upper lip. This center cleft is a shallow depression that runs vertically between the bottom of the nose the upper edge of the upper lip. It is present in virtually all faces between the upper lip and the nose, though its extension below the lower lip is not always obvious, since below the lower lip it is expressed as a horizontal cleft.

To carry out this operation, use a curved gouge — I recommend either a 3/16" veiner or something closely similar to it — to make the center cleft between the upper lip and the nose. Next, using this same type of gouge (or carefully using a knife), form the curved depression that continues the line of the first

43

depression beneath the lower lip and the chin (see Figure 5-9). This lower groove is most prominent in the center of the chin and becomes almost flat toward the outer corners of the mouth, where there is some fatty tissue in the lower chin.

Figure 5-9

Once the mouth is carved, you can start to shape the chin, the jaw, and the neck. On this particular carving, the ears are covered by the head-dress, but the jaw line goes from the chin to the hinge, or joint, located at the ear. It may help to draw in the jaw line on both sides. To get the jaw to stand out,

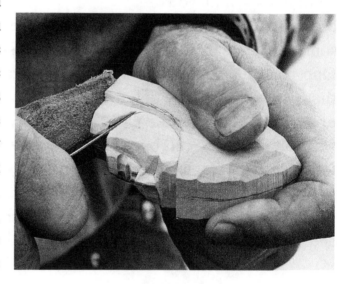

Figure 5-10

follow the reference lines of the jaw and carve the neck narrower (see Figure 5-10).

44

Most people are too conservative in carving the neck area of human heads, and most carvers therefore leave too much wood there. It may help you to keep in mind that the only bone structure in the neck area is the spinal column; everything else in this region is flesh and muscle. Thus, anatomically, the neck is naturally narrower than the skull. So, when you carve a neck, make it narrower than the skull, and provide for some blending curvature between the jaw and the neck.

Before carving the eyes, you can add some character and shape to the cheeks. Native American faces often have high cheek bones. This appearance can be achieved by carving inward and downward (see Figure 5-11), making the cheek bones appear more prominent and perhaps a little higher and bolder than they do on other faces.

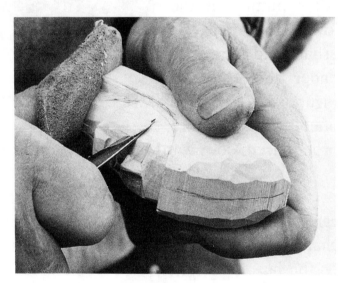

Figure 5-11

Finally, as on the previous head, it is time to put in the eyes. Once again, draw in the shape of the eyes with a pencil, being careful not only to get their size and shape right, but also to place them on the same level and to make them symmetrical with one another.

On the Native American head, I tend to give the eye a more somber expression by dropping the upper lid a bit and by arcing the lower lid downward a bit. After putting in the lower lid line, I usually add extra lines under the eye (see Figure 5-12) and I often put in more pronounced, downward-directed squint lines.

Figure 5-12

Also, using the V-parting tool, other lines of weather and age can be added to the native American Indian face to give it more character. Keep in mind, however, that when paint or stain is put on the face, these lines will become much more apparent, so you will need to be careful not to make them too prominent.

To finish this face, carve in the eyebrows, following the same general procedure that we outlined in Chapter 4 for carving the eyebrows of the wizard's head.

Once you have finished carving the face itself, you may want to return to the headdress and add detail to the bonnet and its feathers. You will probably want to draw in lines outlining the feathers. Then, using the V-parting tool or by making V cuts with your knife, you can make the feathers stand out individually (see Figure 5-13).

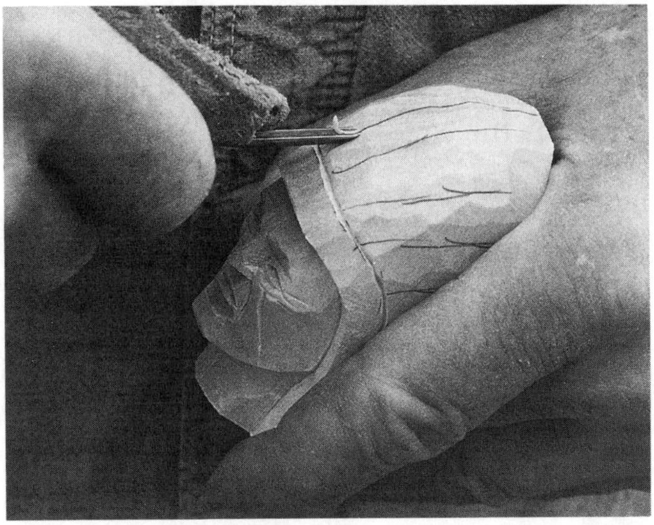

Figure 5-13

On the sides and back of the head, if you have not already done so, you can cut in around the outline of the arc of the bonnet and carve that out. However, you'll want to be careful not to break the tips of the feathers during this operation, since they are often quite thin and fragile.

And that's it. Congratulations! You've finished carving your second face, a native American Indian head.

* * *

Once again, I suggest that you go back over the steps involved in the project. In review, the steps for carving a male head without facial hair are:

1. Give the head an oval shape by cutting off the corners and rounding the head somewhat. However,

47

on this particular carving, notice that you need to round off only the front of the head, due to the shape of the headdress.

2. Establish the shape of the headdress all the way around the face.

3. Block in the nose and eyebrows, following the same general procedure you used for this step in carving the wizard's head in Chapter 4.

4. Shape the nose by taking the corners off the bottom of the nose, taking material off either side of the nose to give it its basic shape, and establishing the shape of the nostrils on either side.

5. Cut in the lines on either side of the mouth area, and carve this area to establish the arc of the mouth and the shape of the cheeks on either side.

6. Draw in and carve the shape of the lips, then shape the area below the mouth and the chin.

7. Shape the jaw and the neck, making the neck narrower than the head.

8. Draw in the shape of the eyes and carve them in, adding lines to define the lower lid.

9. Add lines around the eyes and in other parts of the face to give the face more expression and character.

10. Add whatever amount of detail you wish to put on the headdress.

Side, Front & Top Views of Adult Female Head.

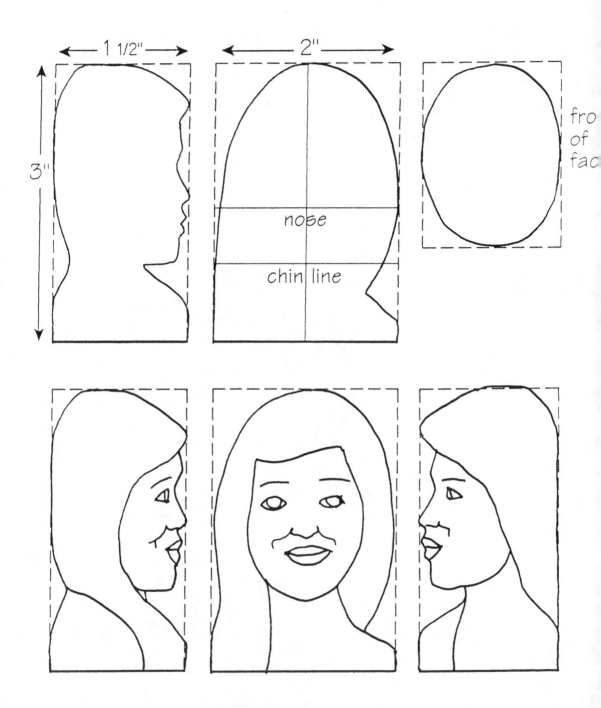

1 1/2"

2"

3"

nose

chin line

fro
of
fac

Chapter 6
Carving a Female Head

Before starting to carve a female head, a few general observations about some of the differences between the male and the female head may be helpful, keeping in mind that these differences are fairly subtle.

One of the differences is that male features generally are broader than female features. For example, male noses tend to be larger and more prominent than female noses. Also, the eyes of males usually are set a little deeper than are those of females (or at least they appear to be set deeper because of the heavier bone structure of the forehead). Also, the male jaw often is somewhat broader than the female jaw, and a man's neck generally is thicker than a woman's. However, while a woman's features generally are more delicate than a man's, a woman's eyes and lips may appear proportionately larger while actually being the same size as a man's, because of the relative petiteness of the surrounding facial structures.

In carving a female head, I try to make such features as the nose and the forehead more rounded, as opposed to angular and jutting. Also, unless one is carving a very old woman, it makes the face more realistic to diminish some of the lines around the eyes and on the cheeks and forehead.

In all honesty, I have to admit that I probably spend twice as much time carving a female face as carving a male face. That may be partly just a matter of practice (I probably carve ten or fifteen male heads for every female head I do, just as a matter of sheer demand). However, I think some of it has to do with the demands I place on myself. I am much more critical of the female heads I carve, perhaps because I approach the task more seriously and with greater expectations. I have discussed this issue with colleagues and some of them admit to the same experience.

I don't mention this with any intention of trying to discourage you from carving female figures. In fact, I enjoy carving female figures in part because they represent more of a challenge to my abilities.

The female head I have chosen to demonstrate here has long hair, with the hair pulled over to one side of the head. Thus, when you take the corners off the blank, you should take very little off the side the hair is pulled to (in this case, the right side), and you should make the front a bit more rounded (as opposed to oval) to allow for the hair. This proportion is also reflected in the initial shape of the blank; unlike the blanks for the two male heads, this blank is somewhat wider than it is thick, as can be seen in Figure 6-1 below.

First, draw in the lines for the hair on the front and on both sides, and also draw in the lines for the nose and eyebrows. Note that, on a female face, the lines where the nose and brows join tend to be much more curved than on a male face.

Next, carve in the hairline (see Figure 6-1). This may have to be done with a series of rather deep stopcuts, because the hair stands out for a considerable distance from the sides of the face.

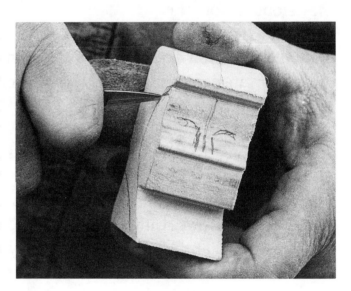

Figure 6-1

Put a part in the middle of hair, but carry the part only as far as the back of the top of the head. In shaping the left side (the side that the hair pulls away from), you should carve in from that side to form the side and front of

53

the neck, allowing the long hair on the right side of the head to stand out above the surface of the neck on the right side (see Figure 6-2).

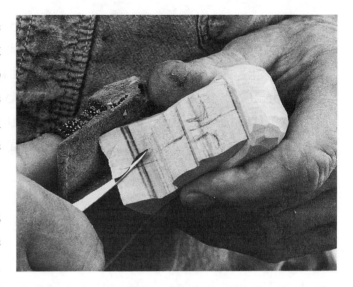

Figure 6-2

The third step is to block in the nose and form the brows. In doing this, make the stopcut for the nose and the brow a continuous curved line on both sides, in contrast to the more angular arrangement in a male face. Also, note two other things in making these stopcuts:

1. Don't go as deep with these cuts as with the male face.

2. Try to put as much as a forty-five degree angle on the cut for the brows, with an upward sweep. This will make the eyes appear to be much less deeply set. Then remove the wood on either side to form the cheek area.

As with your male faces, next take a bit of an angle off the bottom of the nose on either side. Note that there is (or should be) a slight upturn to the bottom of the female nose. You'll want to retain that upturned angle when you take off the corners.

Now carve material off both sides of the nose to give it its proper V shape as seen from above (see Figure 6-3), but round both the bridge and the front of the nose somewhat so as to soften and lighten its appearance.

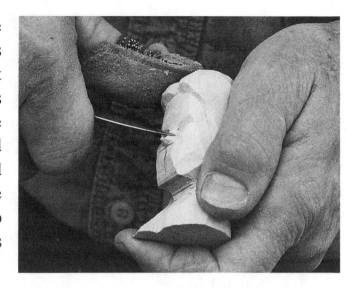

Figure 6-3

Next shape the nostrils. Once again, these features should not be as pronounced or sharp as they would be on a male face. As you can already see, in carving a female face it is important to use a lighter touch and to devote some time and attention to the task of softening the lines of the face by rounding the edges of the features; one way to help to do this is by not taking away as much wood at a time.

The next step is to establish the position of the mouth and to begin forming the cheeks. In doing so, you will follow essentially the same procedure as you did when carving the unbearded male head.

Begin by drawing in the lines for the jowls or smile lines on either side of the mouth. Next, make stopcuts along those lines beginning at the nose and going deeper with the cut as you proceed downward toward the chin. Again, as in carving the unbearded male head, you should shape the cheeks by carving away a little wood at a time on both sides and then round off the mouth area in order to prepare for carving the lips (see Figure 6-4).

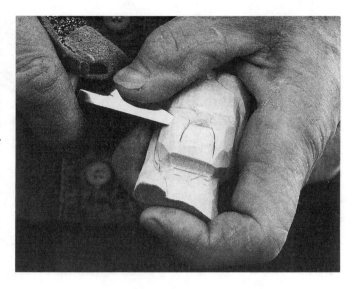

Figure 6-4

In drawing the lips, make them a bit fuller than male lips — that is, they should be a little thicker on both the top and the bottom. If you want to create a smile, the lips should extend further out to the sides, with an upward curvature to both sides and perhaps also some thinning of the lips. We'll go into some of the problems of creating different facial expressions in much greater detail in the last chapter of this book; for now it is best to confine yourself to relatively simple and subtle expressions that can be achieved with a minimum of effort.

Again, as in the unbearded male head you carved earlier, the next step in the process is to make a stopcut along the horizontal line between the upper and lower lips. Once that stopcut is in place, you can proceed to carve in the upper lip, beginning to carve from the outside and proceeding toward the center, first on one side and then on the other. As with all other aspects of carving the mouth, it is important that the lips are symmetrical with one another.

Carving in the lower lip is the next step (see Figure 6-5). In carving the lower lip, you should be careful to make it narrower than the upper lip, unless the lips are smiling. Also, unless the lips are smiling, the upper lip should overlap the lower lip slightly at the sides of the mouth

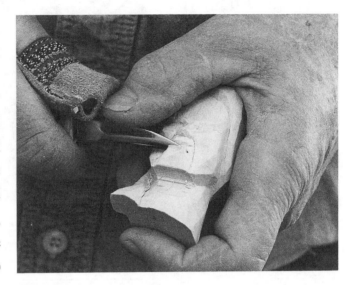

Figure 6-5

(in much the way that the upper lid goes beyond the lower lid of the eyes).

If this is a smiling mouth, then the upper and lower lips should converge at the outside corners, and the amount of curvature in the upper lip should flatten out a bit, making the lips more nearly the same thickness.

Once the lips are carved in and you are pleased with the shape, size and position you have given them, it is time to shape the jaw and the neck. I suggest making the neck even narrower on a female head than you would on a male head. In addition, the jaw of a female head should be more tapered and not as square as in a male, and, by narrowing the cheeks (see Figure 6-6), you will be able to give the face a more mature look; or, by leaving them a bit fuller, you can give the face a more youthful appearance.

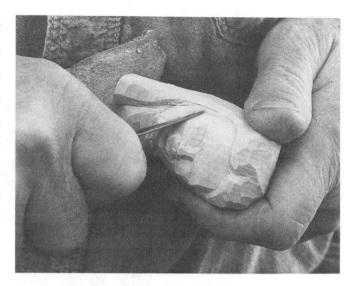

Figure 6-6

Don't forget to carve the indented curvature below the lower lip (see Figure 6-7) and the similar area between the upper lip and the bottom of the nose.

You are now ready to carve the eyes. Once again, we can generalize a bit about the features of a female face. I tend to draw the eyes a little rounder and

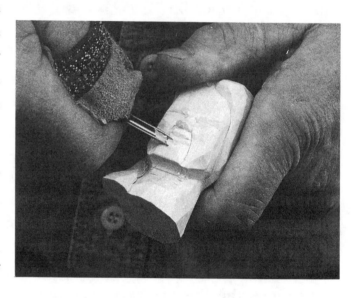

Figure 6-7

perhaps a little more open (thus exposing more of the iris) in female heads, but the facial expression that you are trying to achieve will affect the shape of most of the features of the face (see Figure 6-8). We will discuss all this in much greater detail in Chapter 8.

So, go ahead and draw in the shape desired, and carve the eyes in as you have done previously. As I said earlier, I tend not

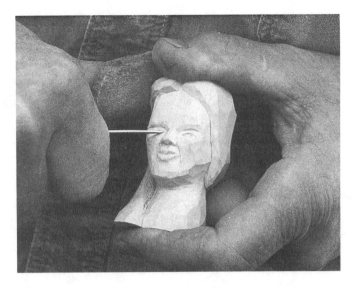

Figure 6-8

to add squint lines or additional lines under the eye (other than the lower eye lid) unless it is an older woman's face. Additional lines seem to add a quality of aging more on female faces than is true on male faces. I suspect that's somewhat cultural.

Finish off the female head by carving in the eyebrows. I usually make them a little thinner and with more curvature than the eyebrows of a male head. If you want texture in the hair, a V-parting tool works well for adding it.

Finally, study your work and touch up and balance the features. When you begin doing various expressions, we will see some of the way in which unbalanced or asymmetrical features can help to convey an expression, but, for now, we want the face to look nice and symmetrical.

*   *   *   *   *

In review, the steps involved in carving the female head are basically the same as those you followed in the first two heads we discussed. Basically they are as follows:

1. Take off the corners of the blank (as seen in top view), aiming for an oval shape to the cross-section of the blank. Notice that a blank for an adult female head should be somewhat wider than it is thick to allow for the extra width required by the hair.

2. Draw in and carve the hairlines, using stopcuts that are considerably deeper than in the preceding two heads because the hair is so much thicker on this female head than on the two previous males ones.

3. Block in and shape the nose, following basically the same steps as in the male heads, but proceeding somewhat more delicately and trying for softer, rounder lines to the surface of the nose.

4. Draw in the cheek and mouth lines and then block in the mouth area. Notice that the jowl or smile lines are somewhat shallower and more curved in a female head than in that of a male.

5. Shape the mouth area, and carve in the lips, again trying for softer, rounder lines to the features.

6. Shape the lower jaw and the neck, and then shape the area under the mouth. The neck should be even thinner in this head than in the male heads you did earlier.

7. Draw in and carve the eyes; then do the eyebrows.

Side, Front & Top Views of Child's Head.

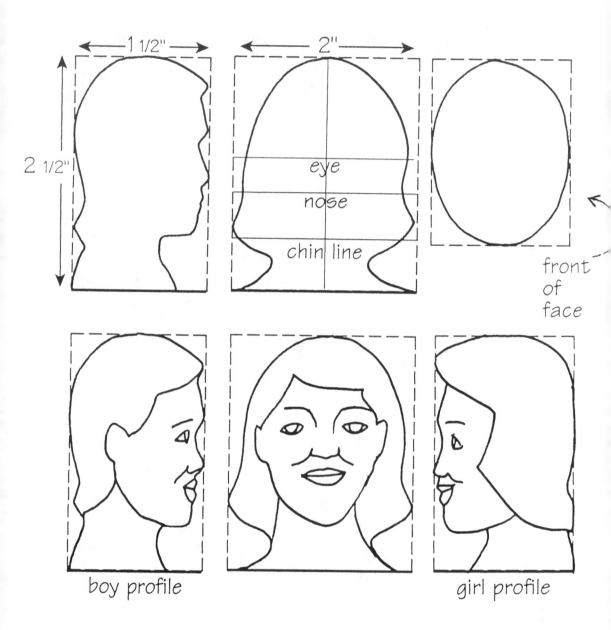

boy profile

girl profile

Chapter 7
Carving a Child's Head

Before you actually start carving a child's head, let me make some general comments that might help to give you some feel for what you are aiming to achieve.

While you will use the same size format for the child's head that you used for the adult heads, there are some important differences. One of these differences is in the proportions. For example, on the adult head, the eyes are situated about halfway between the top and the bottom of the head. On a child's head, the eyes are situated below that center line, approximately two-fifths of the way up from the bottom of the chin. This gives the appearance of considerably larger cranial capacity. The features of the nose and the mouth are smaller and more delicate in a child's head than in an adult's, while the eyes appear larger. The chin is quite a bit smaller and more pointed, while the cheeks are rounder. I really enjoying carving children's faces and find it challenging to bring it off.

In drawing the profile for the blank, note the larger upper head (by comparison with an adult's), the small, almost pug nose, and the upward angle to the bottom of the nose. Notice also that the neck is considerably narrower.

I have drawn two different profiles, one for a girl the other for a boy (see p.62). You have your choice. The only real difference is that the girl's head has longer hair; children's heads and features are basically unisexual for the first few years. You should notice, however, that the head of a child is larger in proportion to the rest of the body than an adult's head. When you go to carve a whole figure, you'll need to take that into consideration, because otherwise the figure will turn out not to look like a child.

As in the first three heads we have discussed, you will start by taking off the corners and rounding the blank, as seen in top view. One slight difference in doing the head of a child is that you want the top view shape to be a little more round as opposed to the more oval shape of an adult's head.

If you choose to do the head of the little boy, it will give you an opportunity to do some ears, and ears can be quite a challenge.

64

For a long time, I avoided including them on my carvings because I found them difficult, but one day I decided that was silly, and just started to carve ears. I cut out a few blanks of heads that would have ears and sat down and carved them. I was determined to figure out a system for carving ears, and it turned out to be much easier than I thought. As a matter of fact, it has turned out to be fun.

You start by drawing the hairline to include short sideburns and the ears. The top of the ear should be even with the eyebrow line, and the bottom of the ear should be even with the bottom of the nose (see p.62). The front of the ear should be at about the midline of the side view of the head.

As in the other heads you have done, your first step is to carve in the hairline (see Figure 7-1); the only difference in the little boy's head is that, in making the stopcuts for the hairline, you make that line go around the sideburn and also around the ears.

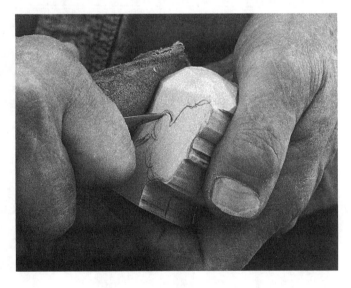

Figure 7-1

Then, when you cut the wood away up to the stopcuts, cut in at a sharp angle around the back of the ear just to relieve the hairline without changing its level much from that of the ear (see Figure 7-2). You block in the basic shape of the ears in much the same way that you block in a nose, except that you want the hairline also to stand out. Thus you cut in at a sharp angle. Once the ears are blocked in and the hairline is established, you can shape the ears. First, cut inward at an angle toward the sides of the face in the front (see Figure 7-3); this will make the ears protrude somewhat from the front to the back.

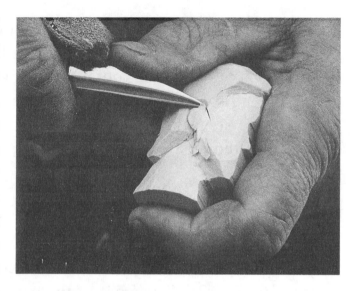

Figure 7-2

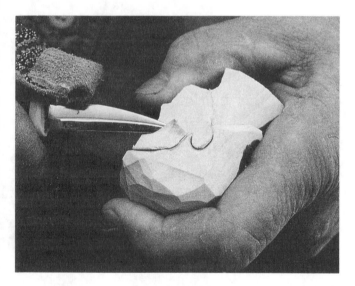

Figure 7-3

Next, shape the interior part of the ear — I usually use a veiner (a U-shaped gouge) to carve in first from the top and then from the bottom to hollow out the sound trap of the ear. On larger carvings that come closer to life size, I usually carve more detail on the interior structure of the ear, but not on these small-scale projects.

As in the previous head, you have carved the features surrounding the face first — in this case, you have done the hairline and the ears. You are now ready to start on the face itself, and, as before, you begin by blocking in the nose and the eyebrows.

On a child's face, the nose does not protrude as much from the face as on an adult's face, and you also want the top of the nose to curve around and flow into the eyebrow lines. Thus, in making the stopcuts, do not cut in as deeply. Make a continuous line from the nose through the eyebrows, then cut the wood out, blocking in the nose. Take off a slight angle on either side of the bottom of the nose, then off the sides.

When you look at the vertical shape of the nose on a child's face, the bridge of the nose is not as prominent as in an adult; its shape is rounder and flatter, so that the nose blends into the cheeks a lot more. I often will use a veiner (a U-shaped gouge) to blend the nose and cheek lines together. The same is true of the eyebrows; they should be fairly shallow and much rounder in shape than in an adult face. Also, though you will want to form the flare of the nostrils as in the adult faces you have already done, you will want to soften them by rounding and blending them to the nose; the nostrils of a child's nose are much less distinct from the rest of the nose than they would be in an adult.

67

To block in the mouth area, draw lines flaring slightly out from the nose, then hooking back around toward the chin (see Figure 7-4). The lines may look a bit distorted at this stage, but these features go into a more compact area in a child's head than in an adult's, and the

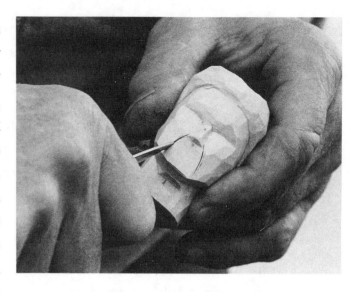

Figure 7-4

curved lines set the stage for rounder cheeks and a somewhat more pointed mouth in a child's head.

Carve out the wood evenly on both sides of the mouth area with the idea of forming nicely rounded cheeks. If we could look down on the mouth area with the nose out of the way, we would see that the mouth curves up to a fairly sharp peak at the midline and then curves downward out toward the sides. You may find that working with a gouge (about a number 5 or number 7) will be helpful in achieving the desired shape in the mouth area.

Now draw in the mouth. You may want to exaggerate the shape of the mouth somewhat when you first carve it in, knowing that you can modify it to a somewhat different shape after it is in place. Next shape the area surrounding the mouth. I tend to exaggerate the center cleft between the upper lip and the nose a bit more on a child's face by carving it in a little more deeply, and I prefer to make the concave area below the lower lip a little more pronounced (see Figure 7-5). Note that, from a profile view, the angle of the upper lip is parallel to the angle of the upward turned nose.

Figure 7-5

In a child's head, the chin should be round but small; the cheeks should be quite round; the neck should be thinner than the neck on any carving we've discussed before, and the jawline should be less rugged and smoother in a child's head than in that of an adult (see Figure 7-6).

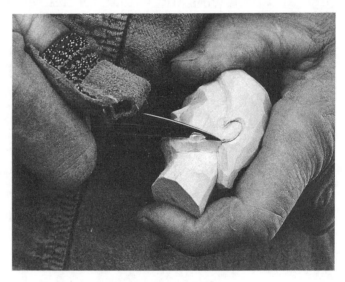

Figure 7-6

However, though the features are smoother, rounder and less rugged in a child's head than in an adult's, the key word in doing children's faces is exaggeration, and the exaggeration is sometimes in opposite directions. For example, you make certain features (the nose, the chin, and the neck) much smaller, while you make the cheeks larger, and you may try to make the eyes appear larger as well. The lips also should have an exaggerated shape, as should the area surrounding the mouth and the chin, and the forehead should be noticeably larger than in an adult. Yet, despite all the exaggeration, the result should come together to read unmistakably as a child's face.

Carving a child's head thus probably will feel awkward at first, and balancing the whole configuration may take a good deal of practice. You probably will have to carve several children's heads before you even begin to feel comfortable and confident about the process and the desired outcome. However, by following the step-by-step method presented here, you should be able to master and enjoy doing this type of carving.

You'll finish up the carving of the boy's head by doing the eyes. Once again, you should exaggerate them a bit by making them proportionately a bit larger and more round and open than in an adult's face. You may find it helpful to try drawing some eye shapes on a piece of paper until you come up with a shape that pleases you and will fit well on the face you are carving. Then draw them onto the carving, and carve them in.

Once you have carved in the eyes and gotten their shape and size right, about the only thing to be added to the shape of the eye itself will be a thin line for the lower lid (see Figure 7-7). Even the eyebrows should be rather subtle and should arch smoothly over the eye.

With that, you have completed the child's head, unless you want to texture the hair. To do so, try using a relatively small veiner. Also, rather than texturing the hair in straight parallel lines, try swirling the tool around using lots of wrist action in order to create a head with curls and locks. This sort of treatment of the hair will add a dramatic finishing touch to the carving (see Figure 7-8).

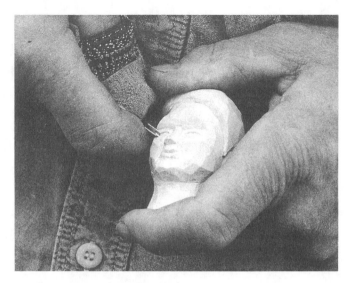

Figure 7-7

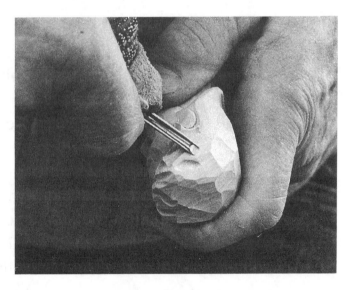

Figure 7-8

71

One very important thing to remember about children's features and heads is that they are basically unisexual. Except for the exposed ears on the head of the little boy and the long hair of the little girl's head, everything else is basically the same.

However, as kids get older, their facial proportions gradually move toward the adult pattern, and I find that capturing the look of kids from the age of about eight through adolescence is the most difficult challenge of all. I often rely more on dress and posture than on facial structure to convey the impression of these intermediate ages.

*   *   *   *   *

In review, the steps you have followed in carving the child's head are much the same as those for adult faces:

1. Round the blank by taking off the corners, as seen in top view.

2. Draw in the hairline (and, on the boy's head, the ears) and carve them all in. Remember to carve out only around the top and backside of the ears, and then carve the angle of the ear in toward the face so that the ear protrudes at an angle from the head.

3. Block in the shape of the nose and the eyebrows, remembering not to go as deeply or as broadly as you would in an adult head.

4. Draw in the cheek and mouth lines and block the mouth in, making the mouth area more pointed toward the center line than you would in an adult face.

5. Cut in and shape the lips, putting in the cleft between the middle of the upper lip and the nose.

6. Shape the indentation below the lower lip, and then carve the jaw and the neck, making the child's neck much narrower than it would be in an adult's head.

7. Draw in and carve the eyes, remembering to make them proportionately larger than in an adult face.

8. Carve the eyebrows in, making them soft (not prominent), and texture the hair.

Chapter 8
Creating Expressions

Once you have mastered the ability to carve a face, the next logical step is to learn to achieve a desired expression. The aim here is to break this process down in such a way as to demystify it and make it possible to create a desired expression deliberately rather than by guesswork and good fortune.

To begin with, a given facial expression is achieved largely by getting all the parts of the face (and the rest of the pose of the figure, if that is relevant) to be saying the same thing at the same time. For example, a smiling mouth should be combined with smiling eyes in order to convey a convincing expression. A smiling mouth and drooping eyes do not combine to make a happy face — it's rather like one person shouting at another, "I'm not angry."

Facial expressions are controlled involuntarily (in most instances) by muscle groups underneath the skin which draw the eyes, the eyebrows, the mouth and the cheeks back and forth and up and down in response to our feelings. I won't attempt to give you an anatomical study of these muscle groups, but I will show you some of the patterns that these muscle groups produce. You will then be able to decide on the kind of facial expression you want to convey on a carving and then deliberately choose among these shapes and produce it.

For the most part, these muscle responses are universal; that is, they are the same the whole world over for men and women, grown-ups and children, all racial groups, and all societies. When humans are happy they smile, when they are angry they frown. When they are not happy they have an expression of sadness. Individuals may learn to control their expressions (for example in a "poker face"), but we usually can tell what people are feeling by the expressions on their faces. As a would-be artist, your aim is to figure out ways of capturing those expressions, so that anyone looking at what you have carved can tell what emotion is expressed there.

To help simplify this, we will combine upper face (eye and eyebrow-forehead) patterns with lower face (mouth, cheek, and jaw) patterns, and then add some of the facial lines that can assist an expression. We'll also combine a few variations of eyes and mouths so that you can begin to see that there can be several ways to create the same expression. I'm sure this could all be reduced to some mathematical formula, but somehow, in my mind, that becomes the dividing line between art and science, and I don't pretend to be a scientist.

There are art books and composite books that give a repertoire of eye, mouth, nose and jaw shapes to choose from, and they can be very helpful in showing the range of individual differences that we see among ourselves — i.e. thick lips & thin lips, wide noses & slender noses, Oriental eyes & European eyes, etc. I refer you to such books to learn more about the variety of facial shapes and features, but what I am after here is to show how the facial muscles act to push or pull the parts of the face into different expressions, regardless of the shape of the specific features being pushed or pulled.

This is not intended as a definitive study of facial expression. Rather, it is a primer aimed at achieving some basic understanding of how the parts of the face interact to produce a particular expression. It's a starting point that will help all your quests into this subject.

Shaping Individual Parts of the Face

As we just mentioned, a particular facial expression depends on the interaction of the individual parts of the face. The problem for the carver (artist) is how to shape each individual part to bring about the desired appearance. In the next few pages, we will consider individual parts of the face (the nose, the eyes, the eyebrows, and the mouth) and show a variety of shapes for each. But always remember, when practicing a particular shape for each facial part, that it is only in combining the parts into a whole that a particular expression is created.

There is an economical way to practice these shapes; take a stick of wood a foot or more in length, and an inch or so square, and practice the shapes using the corner edges. By working on all four sides, you get a lot of mileage out of a single piece of wood, and such practice pieces are dandy references to have around. Harold Enlow uses this approach when he is giving seminars on how to do eyes or mouths.

Eye Shapes

I have found that there are six basic eye shapes that can be used to produce nearly all the expressions used in carvings, though of course there are many subtle variations of each of them. Those six basic shapes are illustrated below.

The NORMAL RELAXED EYE. Note that the curve of the upper and lower eyelids form a elliptical shape with the upper lid extending over the lower lid at the outer corner of the eye.

The HAPPY OR ANGRY EYE. Perhaps somewhat surprisingly, this eye shape works with both happy and with angry expressions. Note that the lower lid curves upward (convexly), while the cheek muscles push the shape upward and outward.

The TIRED OR SAD EYE. This shape can convey either fatigue or sorrow, depending on how it is combined with other features. Notice that both the upper and lower eyelids droop downward, as do all of the facial muscles.

The WINKING EYE. In this pattern, the eye is closed, but the facial muscles draw everything upwards on the side of the face that is winking.

The SLEEPING EYE. In this pattern, the eye is closed, and so the junction between the upper and lower eyelids forms subtle S-shape. The rest of the face is relaxed.

The EVIL OR CUNNING EYE. In this eye shape, both the upper and lower eyelids show a downward curvature. If combined with a lecherous smile, this eye will help to form a wonderful "Jack Nicholson" leer.

Eyebrow Shapes With Eyes

In the following section, eye shapes from the preceding section are combined with different eyebrow/nose combinations to demonstrate some of the different expressions that can be achieved with them. In the descriptions of each of those combinations, we will specify whether the cut underneath the eyebrow is at a steep angle (between 45 degrees and perpendicular) to the wood surface, at a "normal" angle (about 45 degrees), or at a shallow angle (between 45 degrees and nearly flat). Figure 8-1 illustrates each of those cutting angles.

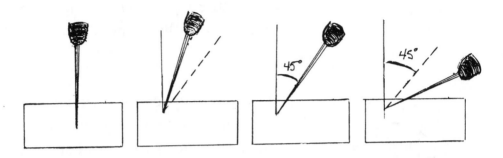

Vertical   Steep   Normal   Shallow

Figure 8-1: Schematic of Various Cutting Angles.

 In a NORMAL/RELAXED expression, use a normal eye and carve a gently curved eyebrow using a moderate cutting angle.

 An expression of DOUBT OR SKEPTICISM involves a happy eye and a more strongly curved eyebrow cut at a shallow angle.

 To create a SAD/GLOOMY expression, use the sad or tired eye and carve a lowered, sloping eyebrow with a steep cut.

79

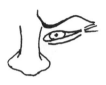

In a FROWN, use the evil/cunning eye with a double curved eyebrow that is carved with a steep angle near the nose that grades to a shallow angle further out.

A WINKING expression involves a winking eye combined with a nearly straight horizontal eyebrow cut at a steep angle.

An expression of SURPRISE can be achieved by combining a normal eye (perhaps a bit more open than usual) combined with a raised (strongly curved) eyebrow carved at a shallow angle.

A SLEEPING expression combines closed (slumbering) eye with a normal eyebrow cut at a moderate angle.

A SMILE involves a happy eye combined with a normal eyebrow cut at a moderate angle.

Mouth Shapes

In this section we will discuss some mouth/lip configurations apart from the other parts of the face. Keep in mind that the interaction of the facial muscles push or pull the parts of the face into different expressions. Those muscles can purse the lips inward or draw them outward. The cheek lines that run down from the margins of the nose on either side of the mouth/lip area will be straight or curved, longer or shorter, and more or less strongly marked depending on the expression being formed. We will see how those lines have to be compatible with mouth/lip shape to achieve a believable expession later.

In a RELAXED mouth, the lips meet at a line that is nearly straight and horzontal and the upper and lower lips are about the same size.

In a SMILE, the lips are still about the same size, though they are drawn outward and meet at a line that is curved upward at both ends; the more the curvature, the stronger the smile.

In an UNHAPPY mouth, the line between the lips curves up from the center and then turns down at both sides of the mouth. The more it curves, the sadder the expession.

A CROOKED SMILE can be achieved by turning one side of the mouth upward (as in a slight smile) and the other side downward (as in a slight frown).

When carving a mouth with the lips closed, start by making the line between the upper and lower lip; cut the line deeper in the center and shallower at the sides. Next cut in the shape of the lips, starting at the outside and cutting back toward the center from either side, being careful that the two sides match.

In a GRIN, the upper lip is thinner than the lower because the sides of the mouth are drawn outward and the upper teeth are exposed.

In a CRYING mouth, the lips are as in a sad mouth except they are thinner and parted to expose the lower teeth and an open mouth.

To carve a mouth that is open with the upper teeth exposed, make the centerline stopcut very deep in the middle, since it is going to be the edge of the teeth. It may be easier to carve in the lower lip before the upper lip, since the upper lip will be raised by another stopcut to expose the teeth. If you want to make the lines between teeth, you can do it either by using a V-parting tool or by cutting a thin V line between the teeth with your knife.

To carve a mouth that is open with the lower teeth exposed, proceed as in the paragraph above, except that you may want to carve the upper lip first, since in this case the lower lip will be raised by another stopcut to expose the teeth.

In a LAUGHING mouth, the lips are more strongly parted, both upper and lower teeth are exposed, and there is a gap between the upper and lower teeth.

Carving a mouth that is wide open, exposing both upper and lower teeth, requires cutting the lines to define the edges of the teeth first, and you should cut them rather deeply. Then make stopcuts for the lips. I prefer to carve the wood away to expose the teeth first, and then to shape the lips.

A PURSED expression may be one of surprise or flirtation; the lips are drawn in toward the center of the mouth and may be slightly opened, with the lines of the upper and lower lips not matching exactly.

A SINGING mouth has the lips parted but no teeth exposed; this is a variation of a relaxed mouth.

 A SHOUTING mouth is open rather wide, with both upper and lower teeth as well as the tongue exposed. The wider the mouth is open, the thinner the lips will be.

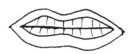 An ANGRY mouth can be achieved by showing the lips parted, the teeth clenched, and the mouth spread out to the side with the lips thinned somewhat.

To carve an open mouth with the teeth exposed but clenched, make the stopcut for the shape of the lips first. Again, I prefer to carve out the area of the teeth before proceeding to the lips. Afterward, cut a dividing line between the upper and lower teeth, and, in separating the individual teeth, note that the lower front teeth are not as large as the upper ones.

Putting the Parts Together Into Faces

We're now ready to consider how the elements we've discussed above can be combined into different overall facial expressions. In studying the examples given below, keep in mind that this is only a small sample of possible facial expressions and that each of them is presented in a highly schematic way in order to discuss the basic patterns involved. Obviously, each of these expressions can be varied in all sorts of ways to achieve different effects.

When you set about trying to apply these ideas about capturing facial expression to your carving, you will find that it is often better to err on the side of exaggeration. A good caricature artist deliberately picks out certain features and exaggerates them to produce a recognizable likeness of an individual, and so it is with expressions. For example, if I carve a man winking one eye, it isn't enough just to carve one eye closed. I need to lower that eye's eyebrow, raise the cheek on that side, and even pull the mouth or the moustache up on that side, and I often execute the carving of those features in an exaggerated way in order to really emphasize the expression.

Many carvers carve the heads for their figures separately and fit them on the body afterward. Most of them admit that their reason for doing so is that if they mess up the face, or don't get the right look, they haven't ruined the whole carving. Others start with the face, so that if they ruin it, at least they haven't invested a lot of time in the rest of the figure.

I suggest cutting out a few blanks and just carving, carving, carving. You should never feel bad about making mistakes, since they are almost always the best teachers. Especially, relish and enjoy those happy mistakes that can sometimes show you a whole new (though sometimes subtle) way of doing something that you hadn't thought of before.

Happy Faces

A "NORMAL" RELAXED EXPRESSION has the eyes open and the cheeks and mouth relaxed. There is no muscle tension pulling or pushing the facial features in any direction.

A "WEAK" OR SLIGHT SMILE has the eyes less open, as the cheeks start to draw up and out. The mouth is drawn out to the sides and turns up slightly at the edges. Dimples may appear and the nostrils are a bit wider.

In a BROAD SMILE the eyes are still less open, the lower lids curve upward, the cheeks are drawn up and out to the limit, and the mouth is drawn up at both edges and out to the point of exposing the front teeth. Dimples and laugh lines are quite noticeable.

In a HEARTY LAUGH, the eyes are almost, if not fully, closed; the mouth is fully open, facial lines are deeply etched, and the nose is even crinkled on the sides. All of the front teeth are exposed — both upper and lower.

Variations on a Smiling Face

A DEVILISH SMILE (*aka* a Jack Nicholson leer) has the eyebrows raised, the teeth exposed and clenched, the lips drawn up in a smiling position, and the cheeks up and out. Crinkles in the nose and a furrowed brow can also help to achieve this expression.

In a PAINED OR INDULGENT SMILE (one perhaps displayed while listening to a piece of music poorly performed), the lips are drawn up in a smile, but the eyes are closed and the brows are drawn inward with a concave dip and some vertical furrows in center of the forehead.

A WINKING OR "KNOWING" SMILE skews the face to the winking side; the lips are noticeably drawn up on that side, as are the nostrils and the cheek on that side, and the eye is closed and the brow flattened. On the other side, the brow may be raised and the eye is open, with a slight convex curve to the lower lid.

In a PEACEFUL OR PIOUS SMILE, there is a nice smile on the lips, the cheeks are drawn up a bit, and the eyes are in a restfully closed position. There are few (if any) lines in the face.

Sad Facial Expressions

A GLUM EXPRESSION has a droopy look — the lips hang down, the eyebrows and eyes sag concavely, the jaw is slack, and even the cheeks sag.

PAINED AND CRYING FACES are quite similar to one another. There is a good deal of tension in the facial muscles which pulls the upper features down and the lower features up. The eyes are squinted with deep furrows, and may even be puffy. While the mouth is drawn out, it is curved downward. The jaw, if not slack, is not set. If there are lines in the face, they are pronounced.

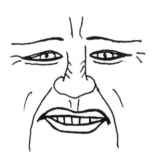

An ANGUISHED EXPRESSION is much like a pained or crying face except that the eyes are slightly more open and the jaw is set with the teeth clenched. There may be anger in this expression.

Expressions of Criticism or Rejection

An expression of PITY OR INDULGENCE may have the lips in an "O" shape, with a slight closing of the eyes and a lowering and scrunching of the eyebrows. The mouth is drawn out, and the cheeks sink in somewhat.

FIRMNESS OR DETERMINATION manifests itself as an expression with the jaw set and jutting out, the teeth clenched, the eyes slightly squinted, and the eyebrows somewhat lowered and furrowed above the nose.

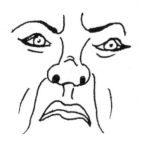

CONDESCENSION OR ALOOFNESS may be expressed with the head tilted back so that the figure is "looking down its nose" with the eyebrows raised, which pulls the upper eyelid up to the outside arc; the mouth is drawn down and the jaw may be drawn in and down.

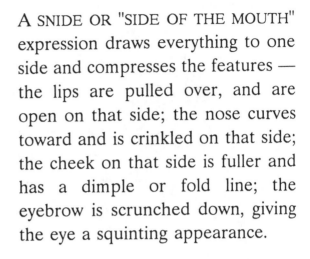

A SNIDE OR "SIDE OF THE MOUTH" expression draws everything to one side and compresses the features — the lips are pulled over, and are open on that side; the nose curves toward and is crinkled on that side; the cheek on that side is fuller and has a dimple or fold line; the eyebrow is scrunched down, giving the eye a squinting appearance.

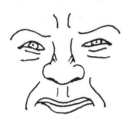

A GLOWER OR FIERCE STARE has the eyebrows frowning, the eyes squinted, the nose slightly flared, and the mouth tense and turned slightly downward with the jaw set. This is an expression of dislike or disapproval.

An expression of SCORN is similar to a glower; it is a fierce look that has a raised eye and eyebrow, a pinched frown to the forehead, a set jaw, and lips turned downward.

OUTRAGE is the ultimate expression of anger — the mouth is open with the teeth bared; the cheeks are pulled outward, narrowing the eyes; the nose is crinkled; the forehead is deeply furrowed; the teeth are clenched; and the jaw is set. There is an aura of violence or threat, and the posture of the figure should also reflect that feeling.

HATRED OR REVULSION is like outrage, but with a feeling of retreat rather than attack. Thus, while the face is quite contorted, all the features are pulled back, as though to say "get away from me" — the eyebrows are pulled up and back; the mouth is pulled back to either side; and the cheeks are drawn outward.

A LOOK OF BOREDOM can be achieved by an upward tilt to the head with the eyes looking up but partially closed, the eyebrows slightly arched, the mouth set in a horizontal line, and the cheeks drawn back and somewhat tense.

92

SURPRISE expressions require an exaggerated widening of the eyes and a raising of the eyebrows; the mouth is drawn outward with the lips open and protruding somewhat to form a rounded "ooooo." There are not a lot of other lines showing on the face.

DISGUST is an expression of extreme distaste — the eyes are squinted; the eyebrows are lowered and clenched; the nose is crinkled; and the cheeks are pulled back and up, which pulls the mouth out to the sides, opening it more on the sides than in the center.

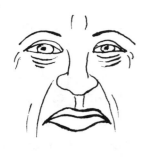

FATIGUE is a droopy expression, especially in the eyes. The upper lids should be relatively deeply outlined, and there are lots of lines under the eyes. The jaw is slack, so the mouth droops, and the cheeks are without tension, so that the cheek lines are straight and shallow.

CURIOSITY has the eyes and the eyebrows drawn upward at the outside. The jaw may be either slack or even drawn downwards giving the face a more elongated narrower appearance.

A LOOK OF PERPLEXION is a combination of questioning and disbelief. The brows are frowning, the eyes squinted with perhaps some crinkle to the nose. The mouth is slightly pursed. The lips protrude.

An INNOCENT "ANGELIC" LOOK is one of roundness; everything seems to curve toward everything else. The mouth curves pleasantly up and the brows curve pleasantly down. The eyes are closed and curved downward. It is a comfortable expression bordering on smugness.

EMBARRASSMENT AND/OR SHYNESS can combine a worried brow and a weak smile. The eyes are averted, probably looking down; the brows pulled in and up in the center, with some furrowing. It is a polite, but pained, look.

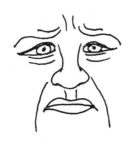

A WORRIED OR ANXIOUS EXPRESSION has a tension with the lips curved down at the outside edges, the eyes squinted, and the cheeks somewhat raised. The brows are pinched in and raised in the center, with some furrows. There should be tension lines, especially under the eyes.

During RESTFUL SLEEP, the facial muscles become slack. The lips may be parted slightly; the eyes are closed, with a relaxed curve. There should be no tension lines.

I have made a real effort to simplify the process of carving facial expressions, but you should realize that carving is like many other skills — you can't really learn how to do it just by reading about it. It's like reading about sailing a boat; much of what you read may make no sense at all until you go out and actually sail. Then, suddenly, the discussion begins to take on real meaning and make sense.

In trying to capture a facial expression, you need to visualize the particular expression clearly, whether in your imagination or from a picture. You then need to think it through in terms of its component parts and then try it. I find it very helpful to constantly keep in mind that it is the facial muscles pulling up or down and in or out on various parts of the face that actually create the expression.

You will probably find that carving facial expressions will make you increasingly observant of people's expressions and of the actions of their facial muscles. Using a mirror to observe your own expressions can also be very instructive.

But you should also always remember that a facial expression by itself is out of context. Facial expressions need the context of "body language." The posture of a figure tells a great deal about the mood being conveyed, quite apart from the facial expression, and when posture and facial expression are combined accurately, the figure takes on a definite meaning. A happy face combined with an erect, energetic posture conveys a mood of joy and leaves no doubt in anyone's mind that "that's a happy figure."

Capturing the nuances of facial expressions can be a complicated and challenging task, and I expect to continue learning about this subject for the rest of my life. However, the discussion in this chapter should make it possible for you master the basics of carving facial expressions and let you proceed from there. Some people seem to have an uncanny, innate ability to do this without much conscious consideration, but I am not one of those folks. I work hard to capture expressions accurately, and I guess I like the challenge. For me, it is real thrill to carve a convincing and meaningful expression, and I hope that it will be for you too.

TO ORDER COPIES OF THIS BOOK:

You can order copies of this book through your local bookstore, through your woodcarving shop, or directly from either the author or the publisher.

To order directly, send payment of $15 for each copy plus $3.50 shipping and handling for up to five copies to one address (Wisconsin residents should add 5.5% sales tax = 83¢ per copy) to the author:

Bob McCurdy
8510 Hwy 57
Baileys Harbor, WI 54202

(414) 839-2754

or to the publisher:

Wm Caxton Ltd
12037 Hwy 42
Ellison Bay, WI 54210

(414) 854-2955 or (800) 288-7724

Wholesale orders should be directed to the publisher; regular trade discount schedules apply to orders from booksellers.